Walter Payton

By
Jane Mersky Leder

Edited By
Dr. Howard Schroeder
Professor in Reading and Language Arts
Dept. of Elementary Education
Mankato State University

Produced & Designed By

Baker Street Productions, Ltd.

*To Josh Kahan,
the best athlete I know.*

CRESTWOOD HOUSE

Mankato, Minnesota
U.S.A.

LIBRARY OF CONGRESS CATALOGING IN PUBLICATION DATA

Leder, Jane Mersky.
  Walter Payton.

  (SCU-2)
  SUMMARY: A career biography of Walter Payton of the Chicago Bears, who
broke rushing records and is known as a "complete player."
  1. Payton, Walter, 1954-   — Juvenile literature. 2. Football players — United
States — Biography — Juvenile literature. 3. Chicago Bears (Football team) —
Juvenile literature. (1. Payton, Walter, 1954-   . 2. Football players. 3. Afro-
Americans — Biography) I. Schroeder, Howard. II. Title. II. Series: Sports
Close-ups.
GV939.P39L43   1986   796.332'092'4   (B)   (92)   86-16526
ISBN 0-89686-318-2

International Standard Book Number:	Library of Congress Catalog Card Number:
0-89686-318-2	86-16526

PHOTO CREDITS

Cover: Mitchell B. Reibe/Sports Chrome
Andy Hoyt/Sports Illustrated: 4, 28
Rick Kolodziej/The F-Stop: 7, 11, 19, 23, 24, 27, 31, 38-39, 42-43, 46
Heinz Kluetmeier/Sports Illustrated: 8, 20, 44
Focus On Sports: 12, 16, 32, 34 -35, 41
Jerry Wachter/Sports Illustrated: 15
UPI/Bettmann Newsphotos: 37

Hwy. 66 South Box 3427
Mankato, MN 56002-3427

TABLE
OF
CONTENTS

Walter Payton did it! On October 7, 1984, he broke
Jim Brown's NFL rushing record.

THEY SAID IT COULD NOT BE DONE

They said it could not be done. They were wrong. On October 7, 1984, Walter Payton did it. The Chicago Bears' star running back broke the record. He passed Jim Brown's total of 12,312 rushing yards. Walter became the National Football League's (NFL) all-time leading rusher. And, for many, Payton was now the most complete player in NFL history.

Walter Payton is fast. He can zip by some of the faster cornerbacks. Payton is quick. He can change directions with the wind. He is strong, too. He bench presses 390 pounds and does sets of leg presses with 700 pounds. He can walk across a football field on his hands.

Payton can also catch the football. In 1984, he led the Bears in catches for the fourth time in six years. What is more, Payton is probably the best blocking back in the NFL. In fact, there is very little that Payton cannot do on the football field.

GROWING UP IN MISSISSIPPI

Walter Jerry Payton was born on July 25, 1954, in Columbia, Mississippi. His mother was a housewife. His father worked in a factory. Walter had a lot of energy as a young boy. "I've always been active," Walter said. "I was born that way."

Walter had a mind of his own. He liked to play tricks on people. His father punished him often. But he also taught his son about being the best. That idea, says Walter, has stuck with him.

Walter's parents were strict Baptists. They led a religious life. They taught their faith in God to Walter. "I told him how I believe everybody's life is preplanned by God," said his mother. "There's no need worrying about it. Whatever's going to happen, is going to happen."

What happened was that young Walter grew up loving music more than he loved sports. He played the drums or anything else he could bang. "He'd come through the house beating on anything he could put his hands on," said his mother. "All he did was drum."

At Columbia High School, Walter was a drummer in the school band. After school he played and sang in jazz-rock bands. He did join the track team. And he set some records in the long jump. He did not play football.

His older brother, Eddie, was the star halfback for the school team. Walter did not want to compete with him. He stayed away from the football team.

"Eddie was always running outside to practice things he'd seen in football games on television," said his mother. "But Walter never did that. He'd just sit and watch. That was all."

When Eddie graduated, the football coach asked Wal-

6

Walter didn't start playing football until he was sixteen, but he has become one of the best players in NFL history.

ter to try out for the team. Walter was sixteen. From the first day of practice, he stood out. He was strong and quick. He became a star in his first game. He ran more than sixty yards for a touchdown!

Walter's high school was integrated in 1970. The black and white school systems in Columbia, Mississippi were combined. Walter's coach remembers the first football game after Columbia High was integrated. "We played Prentiss High and beat them 14-6. Walter had the two touchdowns for us, one of sixty-five yards and the other, ninety-five yards. That did it for integration. Those people in the stands didn't see a black boy running with the ball. What they saw was a Columbia Wildcat."

Walter played two years of great football for the Columbia Wildcats. Colleges all over the country wanted him to play for their team. Walter thought about going to Kansas State University. The school had offered him a football scholarship. He finally decided to follow his brother and go to Jackson State University.

The two brothers played on the same team. Walter soon proved himself to be a better player. He could punt, pass, and run. He scored 464 points after four seasons on the team. No other player in National Collegiate Athletic Association (NCAA) history had ever scored as many points.

Walter was a good student, too. He earned a degree in special education in three-and-a-half years. He graduated at age twenty.

He loved to dance. He and a girlfriend were finalists in a "Soul Train" TV dance contest. Even today, Walter says he wants to dance when his football days are over.

In his last year of college, Walter started an unusual training program. He trained in sand. Walter found a sandbank by the Pearl River near his home. He laid out a course of about sixty-five yards. He had to run in and out and over things. He ran the course five, sometimes ten times. Running on sand is much harder than running on a football field. He wanted to be very strong.

Sometimes the sand got too hot. "Running alone is the toughest," said Walter. "You get to the point where you have to keep pushing yourself. You stop, throw up, and push yourself again. There's no one else around to feel sorry for you."

Walter also ran up and down a bank called The Levee on the same river. Sometimes he did it twenty times in a row. Up one side, down the other. Real short, choppy steps that made his thighs burn. "I tried to run with other people," he said. "But after one or two days, it was tough finding anyone."

Larry Pillers, an ex-San Francisco 49'er, came to work out with Walter one summer. He remembers going with Walter to run the stadium steps at Jackson State University. "The steps went straight up," said Pillers. "I'd do it once. I was through. But Walter just kept going. Walter

Walter (right) and Eddie Payton pose for a picture
with their mother in 1984.

would run up and down the steps for thirty-five minutes without stopping. Then he would rest for five minutes and start again."

"I'd do it until my legs were so tight I couldn't lift them," said Walter. "I guess between May and June I ran close to 700,000 steps."

SWEETNESS

Walter got his nickname, "Sweetness," at Jackson State. His teammates called him "Sweetness" because he had "sweet" moves. Many people felt his nickname should have been "Toughness." Walter liked to run over other players on the football field. Sometimes it seemed that he went out of his way to run right at a defender. "The thing about defensive players," said Walter, "is that they want to hit you as hard as they can. My coach at Jackson State always said, 'If you're going to die anyway, die hard.' So that's what I try to do."

Walter averaged more than 6 yards per carry in college. He also punted, and kicked field goals and extra points. He returned kicks, and completed 14 of 19 passes. He probably should have won the Heisman Trophy. (The award honors the best college football player every year.) But Jackson State is a small, all-black school. Walter did not get the national attention he deserved.

*Walter still carrys the name, "Sweetness," because of
his smooth running.*

PAYTON AND THE CHICAGO BEARS

However, the Chicago Bears noticed Walter. Payton was the first pick of the Bears in 1975.

His rookie year began slowly. He gained zero yards in his first eight carries. He lost two yards in four pass plays. By the end of the season, he had gained 679 yards rushing. He averaged 3.5 yards per rush, and he led the league as a kickoff returner. Payton did not make the All-Rookie team. The Bears finished with a 4-10 record.

The next year Payton exploded. He rushed for 1,390 yards. He was named the *Sporting News* National Football Conference (NFC) Player of the Year. Only an injury

in the last game stopped him from a chance at the NFL rushing title. He sprained his ankle. He lost his chance to beat out O.J. Simpson's record. As he came off the field, he covered his face and cried. Chicago fans had never seen anything like that before. They were surprised. Payton tried to explain later that he had felt so unhappy. He had had such a great year. Everything had come together, then he hurt his ankle.

After the 1976 season, Payton went home to Mississippi. He worked on a master's degree at Jackson State. He spent time with his mother. He was feeling the pressure of playing professional football. His mother helped him see that all he could expect was to do his best.

In 1977, Payton paced the Bears to their first winning season (9-5) in ten years. Payton led the NFC in yards rushing with 1,852. He averaged 5.5 yards per carry. That was his career best. He set a new NFL single-game record for most yards in a game. He gained 275 yards against the Minnesota Vikings.

Payton was proving himself. He seldom could be tackled below the waist. He also made it hard for the defense to flow with the play. He would cut back and go the other way.

After the 1977 season, sportswriters asked Payton when he thought he was going to break Jim Brown's all-time rushing record of 12,312 yards. "I won't be around long enough," he said. "Five years is plenty in this game." Little did he know what the future would bring!

Walter plays in jersey number 34 for the Chicago Bears.

PAYTON MAKES IT BIG

Payton was a star. He had proved his ability with the Chicago Bears. The Bears wanted to pay him enough money to keep him happy. They gave him three contracts, one for each of the next three years. He would earn an estimated $400,000 in 1978, $425,000 in 1979, and $450,000 in 1980.

The 1978 Bears had a new coach. His name was Neil Armstrong. Under Armstrong, Payton and teammate Roland Harper were the best pair of running backs in the NFL. The two players gained seventy-two percent of the Bears' yardage. Payton made the longest run of his career. He ran for 76 yards against Denver. Three days later, he set his career record for the most yards as a receiver in one game — 119. He caught fifty passes for the season. And he was named to the Pro Bowl as a starter.

Payton's teammates and coaches liked and admired him. "Walter is like a young kid," said teammate Ted Albrecht. "We all have some of the little kid in us, but he has more than normal. I think it's beautiful."

Players from other teams respected him, too. O.J. Simpson described Payton as an "insane" runner. "There is no rhyme or reason to what he does," said O.J. "But it all works out."

Payton agreed. "I guess my running comes by instinct. I don't try to define it or explain it . . . only improve it."

Payton kept improving. He gained 1,610 yards on the

Walter was best rusher in the NFC for five straight years.

ground and scored 13 touchdowns the next season. He got the chance to pass the football twice. The first pass was caught for fifty-four yards. The second pass was caught for a touchdown. Payton was again a Pro Bowl starter. And he was voted to the all-NFC team. He did all of this with a painful injury in his shoulder.

"The guy is amazing," said Chicago Bear Doug Plank. "Week after week I see him put his head down and hit guys in the chest, and **they** get carried off. He's doing things nobody else could have done."

In 1980, Payton won the NFC rushing title for the fifth year in a row. He gained 1,460 yards. No other football player had been the best rusher for five years straight in the NFC.

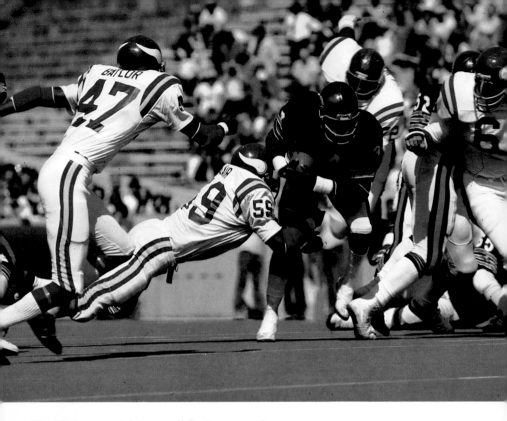

The 1981 season didn't go well for Payton or the Chicago Bears. Walter complained about the poor blocking he was getting.

BAD TIMES

The next season, Payton and the Bears ran into some bad luck. The Bears finished last in their division. Payton gained only 1,220 yards, the fewest since his first season. He failed to win the NFC rushing title for the first time in five years.

After the Bears' third game, Payton had told the sportswriters how he felt. He was upset. His blockers were not blocking for him. He was not gaining the yards he should have gained. "It got to the point where there wasn't any place to go," he said.

A week later, the Bears had lost to the Los Angeles Rams. Payton gained only 45 yards in 17 carries. His shoulder hurt. He was tired. Someone reminded him that he had once given some of the Bears' players gold watches for their excellent blocking. "This year I'll give them pieces of my body," he said.

Payton now knew he was going to have to keep his body and mind fit. He would have to stay sharp. He learned he could not always count on the other players to play their best.

BROWN'S RECORD WITHIN REACH

At the start of the 1982 season, Jim Brown's rushing record was in reach. Payton had already rushed for 9,608 yards. He needed 2,705 more yards to break Brown's record. "I'm a little less than 400 yards away from 10,000," he said. "I can get the record with two 1,400-yard seasons."

The 1982 season was shortened because of a players' strike. Payton gained only 596 yards rushing. That was far less than the 1,400 he had hoped for. The Bears, under new coach Mike Ditka, did not do much better. They won only three of their nine games.

After the season, the Bears signed Walter to a new

contract. He would earn $240,000 a year for no fewer than forty-three years! It was the most expensive contract in NFL history.

Chicago Bears' fans were thrilled. They had worried that Payton might sign with a new Chicago team called the Blitz. The Blitz was in a new league called the United States Football League (USFL).

The President of the Bears, Michael McCaskey, fell to his knees and bowed in front of Payton when he signed again with his team. The Bears needed Payton badly. He had been the only star for nine years. He had started 120 games in a row. He sat out only one of 131 games in his career. The Bears' president put it this way. "If you ask what the Bears stand for, you have to say Walter Payton."

And what did Payton say he stood for? "I'd like to be remembered as a guy like Pete Rose. Somebody who stands for hard work and total effort. I want to do everything perfectly on the field."

Payton was on his way to becoming the most complete football player in history.

HARD TRAINING PAYS OFF

Payton knew he had to train hard before the '83 season. He had turned twenty-nine. "I feel like an old man," he said. He did not look like one. His face had no lines. He moved quickly.

*Although he is in very good shape, even Walter gets
tired during a game.*

In the early days, he had trained in Mississippi. He ran in the sand. He ran up the bank of the river. He ran up and down stadium steps. Now he ran up "The Hill" near his new home in Illinois.

"The Hill" does not look like much from a distance. It seems to go straight up when you stand right next to it. The only way to get up "The Hill" is with cleats. You cannot make it in sneakers.

Payton ran up "The Hill" every day. If he missed a day, it was like starting all over. Four times up and down was enough at first. The most he ever did was fifteen in a row. "The hardest workout I ever had was running three-and-

a-half miles to "The Hill," ten times up and down, and then three-and-a-half miles back home."

The power in his legs made Payton strong. It was his base of strength. He got it from "The Hill." "I've got to keep my body and mind together so everything will be sharp."

Payton's training paid off. He rushed for 1,421 yards in 1983. He caught passes for 607 yards. That was the most catches (53) of any Bear. He passed for 95 yards. He gained a total of more than 2,000 yards for the second time in his career. His yardage was thirty-six percent of the Bears' total yardage. He was almost a one-man team.

The wear and tear took its toll on Payton. In the spring of 1984, he had surgery on both of his knees. Would he come back? Could he beat Brown's record?

THE RECORD IS HIS

The 1984 season started out well for the Bears. They won their first three games against Tampa Bay, Denver, and Green Bay. But the Seahawks put a stop to the winning streak in Game 4. They beat the Bears 38-9. Though Payton ran for 116 yards, the Seahawks were too much for the Bears. They stopped them cold. Game 5 did not go well, either. The Bears lost to Dallas 23-14.

But with fourteen minutes to go in the third quarter in Game 6 against the New Orleans Saints, Payton had a

Walter works hard to stay in shape.

chance to pass Jim Brown for a new NFL rushing record.

It was Payton's second carry of the second half. The ball was on the Bears' 21-yard line. Chicago was ahead 7-3. A gray sky threatened rain. There was nothing special about the play. The Bears had used it hundreds of times.

At the snap, the left tackle and the tight end blocked out a Saints' player. Left guard Mark Bortz pulled. Dennis McKinnon and Matt Suhey led into the hole. Payton ran along the backfield. He held the ball like a potato in his right hand. He looked over the scene before him. Then he tucked the ball under his arm, squared his shoulders, and ran for the record.

He gained six yards. He increased his rushing total to 12,317 yards. That was five more than Brown gained in his nine seasons. At that moment, Payton became the top runner in the history of football. The hometown Chicago fans went wild!

For weeks Payton had tried not to get nervous. Before the Dallas game the week before, he almost passed out. "I've never felt like that before," he said. "It sort of scared me."

He had needed 221 yards in the Dallas game to beat the record. But in the Cowboy's history only one person had ever run more than 200 yards against them. That was Jim Brown. Payton gained 130 yards in the first half against Dallas. But for some reason, he only carried the ball five times in the second half. He ended the game with 155 yards. That made him sixty-seven yards short of the record.

Payton broke Jim Brown's NFL rushing record in a game against the Saints. It was a very special day for Walter.

22

Payton studied films of Brown. "Brown was big and strong and quick," he said. "And he even made a catch with one hand. That's what football is all about. That, and staying healthy." Payton knew about good health. He had not missed a game in 126 starts.

Brown was nowhere in sight when Payton broke his record. In the months before Payton's historical run, Brown had been making a fuss. He talked a lot about Payton and the other players closing in on his record. He discussed whether he thought they were worthy of a place in football history. The Bears' management thought it would be best if Brown did not attend the game. They wanted the day to belong to Walter.

And it did. He ran for 154 yards against the Saints, for a grand total of 12,400 yards. It was the fifty-ninth time that

Every time Walter carries the football, he sets a new NFL rushing record!

he had run for over 100 yards. Payton now held twenty-one Bears' records. After the game, he led the NFL in rushing with 775 yards. He was off to the best start of his career after six games.

"He's going to put the career record so far out there, that yours truly won't have a chance," said Tony Dorsett. Dorsett is the player thought to have the best chance of passing Payton someday.

When Payton passed Brown's record, he wanted the game to go on. That was impossible. People ran onto the field. Payton dashed to the Saints' sideline. He shook hands with coach Bum Phillips. Then he ran away from the mob and cut to the Bears' sideline. He handed the ball to one of the Bears' coaches, Johnny Roland. Roland took it to Pete Elliott who used to head the NFL Hall of Fame. The ball would go on display at the Hall of Fame until the end of the season.

Payton earned a $100,000 bonus for breaking the record. He also got a $125,000 Lamborghini Countach-S car from the Kangaroo Shoe Company.

"So far, people have never tried to just hurt me," said Payton. "And I guess that's because of the way I play." That explained why even the Saints applauded when he broke the record.

After the game, Payton talked to President Reagan on the phone. "The check is in the mail," he said to the President. Everyone laughed. Payton had let the President know that he would be paying his 1984 taxes on the bonus and the car.

ONE MORE GOAL: TO WIN THE SUPER BOWL

Payton had broken Jim Brown's record. He had one more goal. He wanted to play in a Super Bowl. He had been with the Bears for ten years. Not once had the team made it to the Super Bowl.

His good friend, Matt Suhey, put it this way. "He's got the records. He's got a good life. He's made lots of money. But he hasn't got the ultimate: To win the Super Bowl."

The Bears finished the 1984 season with a 10-6 record. They played the Washington Redskins in the divisional play-offs and won 23-19. Payton rushed for 104 yards in that game, caught one pass, and threw for another.

The Bears were excited. Maybe they could make it to the Super Bowl. They played San Francisco in the NFC championship game. They lost 23-0. Payton was held to 92 yards, a bad day for him. The offense could not get going.

The Bears would have to wait to fulfill their Super Bowl dream.

1985-86: THE SUPER SEASON

The Bears played the Tampa Bay Buccaneers in the first game of the 1985-86 season. They fell behind. But they came back to win 38-28. The win set the tone for the rest of the year. The Bears were a new team. They were winners.

Walter cuts up the field in an early 1985 game.

Payton and the Bears were on the move!

The Bears beat the world champion San Francisco 49ers in week six of the season. The win put the Bears above .500 for the first time in Payton's career. In 153 games since he arrived, the Bears were now 77-76.

Payton also passed the 14,000-yard rushing mark during the San Francisco game. Each yard he gained was history. But each win was the only important thing. "Right now," Payton said, "I'm just happy to be in this situation." The Bears were winning. That was all that counted.

The Green Bay Packers played the Bears next. The Packers were mad. The Bears had beaten them two weeks before on Monday-night television. The Packers wanted revenge.

On the eighth play of the game, a Packers' player forced Payton out of bounds and over the Bears' bench. The Packer player was thrown out of the game. The Packers got three more personal fouls for rough play in the first half. The Bears were behind 10-9.

Then Payton went to work. He gained 192 yards by the time the game was over. It was his best game in seven years.

"He's the best football player I've ever seen," said coach Ditka. "At any position."

SUPER BOWL BOUND

The Bears won their first nine games. They were the only team in the NFL left without a loss. They were everybody's No. 1 team.

In Game 10, the Bears' defense held the Detroit Lions to only 106 yards. The defense was strong and good. During the season, they had allowed the least number of points of any NFL team.

On November 17, the Bears met the Dallas Cowboys. The Bears played the Cowboys without Jim McMahon, their best quarterback. The last time they had beaten Dallas was in 1971. Tickets for the game went for as much as $250.

The Bears were excited when they walked onto the football field. They had a good feeling about the game. What happened was almost too good to be true.

The defense scored the first two touchdowns. The offense took it from there. Payton gained his usual yards. The Bears won big, 44-0. Nobody had ever beaten the Cowboys that badly. The Bears had clinched the NFC Central Division title. It was their eleventh win in a row. It was the earliest a team had ever won a Division title.

The Bears laughed about the game. And they laughed about the play with Payton and William "The Refrigerator" Perry. Perry weighed 308 pounds. No one could miss him when he was in the game.

Payton leaps high for a touchdown!

The Bears were on the Cowboys' 2-yard line. Perry was sent into the game. He went in motion and blocked for Payton. Payton got to the 1-yard line, then he was stacked up by several Cowboys. Perry jumped off the ground. He grabbed Payton and tried to carry him into the end zone. It is illegal to help a runner that way. The Bears got a 10-yard penalty.

"I was trying to pull some of those people off him," said Perry. "When I got to Walter, I wanted to help him, too." When Perry got to the sideline, his teammates told him the rules. "They told me I couldn't do that, but I was just having fun."

Coach Ditka joked, "Next week, we put Payton on his shoulders." Then he gave every player on the team a game ball.

Everyone was talking about the Bears. Tampa Bay coach, Bennett, said there was "No question" the Bears were the best team in football. "You don't know whether to defend against the run or the pass," he said.

San Francisco coach Bill Walsh said the Bears' defense was so good that it "depressed" him to think about it.

Green Bay coach Gregg said the Bears "Could be the best team in this league in the last ten years."

The Bears were on top of the world. They enjoyed every minute. "If we play like we can play," said Jim McMahon, "ain't nobody who can beat us. Maybe last year we had some doubts. But not anymore."

A LOSS TO MIAMI

Jim McMahon said no one could beat the Bears. Their record was 12-0. Then they played the Miami Dolphins on December 2. The game was seen by millions on Monday-night football.

Miami's quarterback Marino completed 14 of 17 passes for 270 yards and three touchdowns. The Dolphins scored the first five times they got the ball. They took a 31-10 lead at half time.

It was too late for the Bears. The Miami fans counted down the last seconds of the game. Their 1972 team would remain the last unbeaten team. The Bears lost, 38-24.

"Nobody's perfect," said coach Ditka, "and we proved it. Now it's what you do with it. Do you bounce back? We'll be back."

Payton still had a good day. He got his eighth 100-yard game in a row. He finished with 121 yards.

The Bears knew they might play the Dolphins again in the play-offs. "We gave them 21 points," said Payton. "But we might play these guys again. It was a good experience."

Chicago fans were unhappy. They had wanted a perfect season with no losses. Their unhappiness did not last for long.

After beating Dallas, the Bears felt like they were on top of the world!

*Payton and the Bears handed the Cowboys their worst
loss ever — 44-0.*

ON THE WAY TO
THE PLAY-OFFS

The Bears bounced back from the Miami loss and beat the New York Jets the next week. However, the Jets held Payton to 53 yards. They stopped him eleven times for losses or no gain. They ended his string of 100-yard games. But the Bears won by going to the pass.

"A lot of teams try to stop the run," said Payton. "Then we burn them on the pass. I'm not disappointed at not getting 100 yards."

The Bears' next game was against the Detroit Lions. The Bears had beaten them 24-3 earlier in the year. Payton had rushed for more than 100 yards in that game.

The Bears started slowly. It took a fifty-yard pass by Payton to Willie Gault to finally get the offense into the end zone. But the Bears pounded the Lions in the fourth quarter, scoring twenty-one points. They beat the Lions 37-17. Coach Ditka was not impressed, however. "We couldn't beat a play-off team today," he said. "We would have been eliminated." Ditka knew the Bears had only two weeks to get ready for the play-offs. He was worried. The Bears were not playing their best ball.

Many players disagreed. "We're where we want to be," said Mike Singletary. "In two weeks, I think we're going to get out there and play great football."

Payton finished the regular season with 14,860 yards rushing. No team had been able to stop him. He ran for a

Walter Payton holds a trophy for being Black Athlete of 1984.

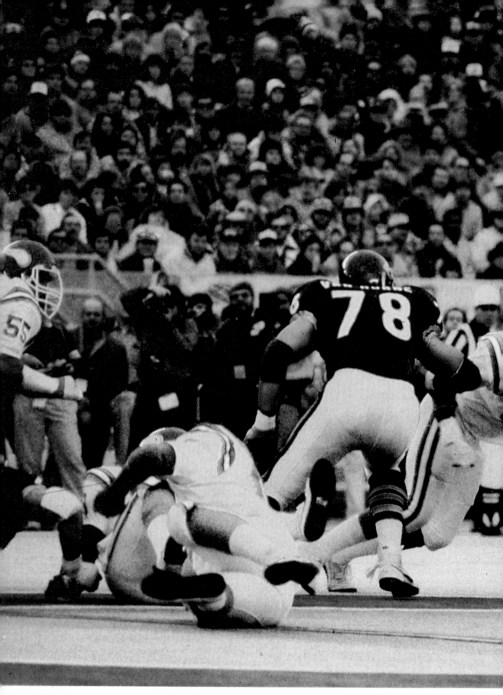

Walter goes through a big hole to score against the
Vikings earlier in the year.

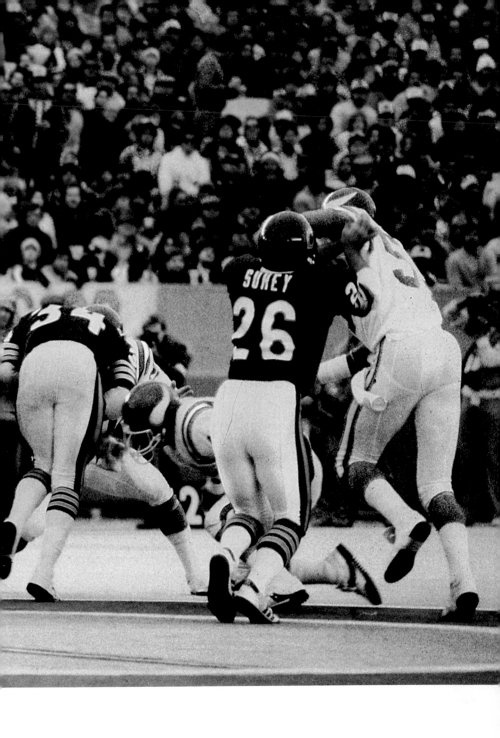

record nine-straight, 100-yard games. He led the team in pass catches. It had been a great season.

PLAYING GREAT FOOTBALL

Payton and the Bears were ready for the play-offs. They played the New York Giants in the NFC semifinals. Before the game, the Giants said they could win. They compared their best running back, Joe Morris, to Payton. Many of the Bears disagreed. "I don't think there's any comparison," said Singletary. "I've not really heard of him before this year," said Otis Wilson.

The Bears were not going to change their game plan. They were going to win **their** way.

And that is what they did. They beat the Giants 21-0. The Bears held New York to an average of 40 inches a play until the end of the game. Joe Morris gained only 32 yards. Payton ran for 93 yards and caught a pass for another four. The Bears outplayed the Giants in every way. They proved they were a great team. Now they had one more game to win. Then the Bears would play in the Super Bowl.

The Los Angeles Rams should have stayed home. Instead, they came to Chicago. The Bears beat them 24-0. The Bears were the only team ever to record two straight shutouts in the play-offs. The Bears were awesome!

After the game, one Bear after another stopped by

Payton and the Bears beat the Rams 24-0.

40

Payton's locker just to touch him. They knew how happy he was to be going to his first Super Bowl.

Payton had had to wait eleven long years to play in the Super Bowl. It did not matter that he had had a bad game against the Rams. (He ran for only 32 yards. He fumbled twice. He dropped a pass.) Payton was going to the Super Bowl! "I can't believe that we're there yet," he said. "I don't know how to act."

His teammates knew how they felt about Payton. "We wanted this for him," said Wilber Marshall.

"For him to go out with all those records, and not go to the Super Bowl, it would have been a crime," said Matt Suhey.

Payton knew the ending had not been written yet. "We have one more thing to do," he said. "Getting there isn't good enough. We have to win."

Walter and a Bears' coach discuss an idea on the sidelines.

Like a lot of people, Walter enjoys fishing when he has some spare time.

WINNING THE SUPER BOWL

A sellout crowd of 73,818 came to New Orleans to watch the Bears play the New England Patriots in Super Bowl XX. They saw the Bears cream the Patriots 46-10. It had been twenty-three long years since the 1963 Bears had won the NFL championship. At last, Chicago and the Bears could chant, "We're No. 1!"

Chicago fans poured into the streets of Chicago. Dreams had come true. Chicago was a winner. Chicagoans jumped for joy.

"Today history was set," said Mike Singletary. "I think we're one of the best teams of all time." The Bears finished the season with an 18-1 record. That matched the 1984 San Francisco 49'ers for the second-best mark in league history. (The Miami Dolphins hold the record, 16-0).

The Bears set Super Bowl records for most points scored, biggest margin of victory, and fewest yards allowed rushing. New England gained only seven yards on the ground.

Sadly, Payton did not score during the 46-10 win. He was disappointed. "I felt bad, but that's the way the game goes. There have been other games when I haven't gotten into the end zone. That's the way the game is played."

Payton did not score in the Super Bowl. But no one could deny his importance to the Bears. He had been the team leader for eleven years. Still, some of his teammates

45

Walter Payton always wants more!

felt bad. "We could be a lot happier than we are," said Dennis McKinnon.

Chicago fans had wished Payton had scored, too. But they knew he was super anyway. He did not need a Super Bowl touchdown to be the greatest!

ANOTHER THREE YEARS

Payton was not giving up. He had played eleven great years of football. He would go on. "I would like to end up with 18,000 yards," he said after the Super Bowl. That meant he had 3,140 yards to go.

"That's right," said Payton. "That means another three years!"

WALTER PAYTON'S PROFESSIONAL STATISTICS

Year	Rushing (Yards/Avg.)	Receiving (Yards/Avg.)	Passing (Yards/Avg.)	Touchdowns
1975	679/3.5	2,213/6.5	0/0	7
1976	1,390/4.5	149/9.9	0/0	13
1977	1,852/5.5	269/10	0/0	16
1978	1,395/4.2	480/9.5	0/0	11
1979	1,610/4.4	313/10.1	54/54	17
1980	1,460/4.6	367/8.0	0/0	7
1981	1,222/3.6	379/9.2	0/0	8
1982*	596/4.0	311/9.7	39/13	2
1983	1,421/4.5	607/11.5	95/16	11
1984	1,684/4.4	368/8.2	0/0	11
1985	1,551/4.8	483/9.9	96/19	12
TOTALS:	**14,860/4.4**	**3,938/9.3**	**284/13.5**	**115**

*8-game season due to NFL strike.